Children with ADD:
A Shared Responsibility

Based on a Report of The Council for Exceptional Children's Task Force on Children with Attention Deficit Disorder

Published by The Council for Exceptional Children

Library of Congress Cataloging-in-Publication Data

Children with ADD : a shared responsibility : based on a report of The
  Council for Exceptional Children's Task Force on Children with
  Attention Deficit Disorder.
      p. cm.
    Includes bibliographical references.
    ISBN 0-86586-233-8
    1. Attention-deficit-disordered children—Education—United
  States. 2. School management and organization—United States.
  I. Council for Exceptional Children. Task Force on Children with
  Attention Deficit Disorders.
  LC4707.4.C55 1992
  371.9—dc20   92-27238
                                                                    CIP

ISBN 0-86586-233-8

Copyright 1992 by The Council for Exceptional Children, 1920 Association Drive, Reston, Virginia 22091-1589.
Stock No. P385

All rights reserved. No part of this publication may be reproduced, stored in a retrieval system, or transmitted, in any form or by any means, electronic, mechanical, photocopying, recording, or otherwise, without the prior written permission of the copyright owner.

Printed in the United States of America
10 9 8 7 6 5 4 3 2

Contents

Foreword, v

Members of CEC's Task Force on Children with ADD, vii

Consultants to Task Force, ix

1. Introduction, 1

The responsibility for meeting the educational needs of children with attention deficit disorder (ADD) does not belong to one segment of the education system, but rather to the education system as a whole.

2. CEC Examines the Issues, 2

CEC Task Force addresses three major perspectives that will shape future services: (1) children with ADD are currently in both general and special education programs; (2) these children are at greater risk of developing learning and/or behavioral problems; and (3) all teachers and administrators want information on how to meet the needs of these children.

3. Prevalence and Characteristics of Attention Deficit Disorder, 6

Between 1.35 and 2.25 million school-age children in the United States may have an attention deficit disorder. Characteristics include developmentally inappropriate degrees of inattention, impulsiveness, and/or hyperactivity.

4. Evaluation, 9

A two-tiered process of evaluation is recommended (1) to determine whether or not a child meets the criteria for diagnosis of ADD and (2) to determine the degree to which the child's educational performance is adversely affected.

5. Prereferral Intervention and Teacher Assistance Teams, 11
Proactive strategies, such as prereferral intervention and the use of teacher assistance teams, help to reduce the risk of underachievement and academic and social failure.

6. Multidisciplinary Approaches and Professional Collaboration, 13
Effective programs use a multidisciplinary approach to meeting the needs of children with ADD and encourage professional collaboration.

7. Communication, 17
Effective programs encourage frequent parent-professional and professional-professional communication.

8. Positive School Climate, 18
Effective programs create a positive school climate and provide the support, flexibility, and continuing education needed by teachers to meet diverse educational needs.

9. Continuing Education and Staff Development, 21
Effective programs provide the continuing education and staff development necessary for successful program implementation.

10. Classroom Strategies That Help Children Focus on Learning Tasks, 22
Effective strategies include seating the student near the teacher; shortening or reducing the difficulty of assignments; teaching learning strategies; using behavioral approaches; teaching social skills; and providing assistance in learning how to organize.

11. Classroom Strategies That Accommodate Different Abilities to Maintain Attention and Keep Activity Within Certain Levels, 24
Appropriate school behavior and learning are dependent on a child's ability to orient, maintain attention, and keep activity within certain levels for extended periods of time.

References, 31

Additional Resources, 33

Foreword

This document should be viewed as a beginning effort to address the educational needs of children with attention deficit disorder (ADD). The contents should be helpful to teachers of both regular and special education classes. Parents and school administrators may find this document helpful as well.

Both the members of The Council for Exceptional Children's Task Force on Children with Attention Deficit Disorder and the consultants to the Task Force should be recognized for their efforts in developing a meaningful report. Dawna Farrar, CEC staff/governmental relations, played a significant role in the Task Force's work. Through her tireless commitment to this project, we were able to have a successful hearing, create the numerous drafts of the report, involve all Task Force members and consultants, and, most important, present this report at this time.

We hope the document will be user friendly and that it will be embraced by the education community as a foundation from which to build, focusing upon the educational needs and successes of children with ADD.

Joseph A. Ovick
Chair, Task Force on Children
with Attention Deficit Disorder

Members of CEC's Task Force on Children with ADD

Joseph Ovick
ADD Task Force Chair
Assistant Superintendent
Student Services
Contra Costa County Office
  of Education
Vallejo, California

Susan Brown
LD Teacher
Kennesaw, Georgia

Elaine Cutler
Principal
Seminole Elementary School
Seminole, Florida

Steve R. Forness
Professor and Director
Mental Retardation and
  Developmental Disabilities
Interdisciplinary Training
  Program
UCLA–Neuropsychiatric Institute
Los Angeles, California

Gay Goodman
Associate Professor
Department of Educational
  Psychology
University of Houston
Houston, Texas

Frank E. Michener
Psychiatrist
Alexandria, Virginia

M. Christine Sivik
Teacher
Ardmore School
Westmont, Illinois

Consultants to Task Force

Patricia Crowe
Teacher, Second Grade
Griswold Elementary School
North Franklin, Connecticut

Mary C. Fowler
Vice President for
 Governmental Affairs
CH.A.D.D.
Fairhaven, New Jersey

Quenton Graham
Clinical Psychologist
Washington, DC

Pam Haugland
Outreach Director
Midwest Children's Center
Rapid City, South Dakota

Desmond Kelly
Assistant Professor of Pediatrics
 and Director, Learning and
 Attention Problems Project
Southern Illinois University
School of Medicine
Springfield, Illinois

Lamoine J. Miller
Professor and Coordinator
 of Special Education Programs
Northeast Louisiana University
Monroe, Louisiana

Phyllis Ollie
Supervisor, Physically
 Handicapped/Health Impaired
Milwaukee Public Schools
Milwaukee, Wisconsin

Susan Osborne
Department of Curriculum and
 Instruction
North Carolina State University
Raleigh, North Carolina

Harvey C. Parker
Executive Director
CH.A.D.D.
Plantation, Florida

Ronald Reeve
Associate Professor of Education
University of Virginia
Charlottesville, Virginia

Mike Rosenburg
Professor of Education
Coordinator of Special
 Education
Johns Hopkins University
Baltimore, Maryland

Jim Swanson
Professor of Pediatrics
Director of Child Development
 Center
University of California at Irvine
Irvine, California

Sandra F. Thomas
President
CH.A.D.D.
Greenfield, Massachusetts

Ron Walker
Teacher Trainer
Southeast Psychological Institute
Atlanta, Georgia

Josephine Young-O'Neal
School Psychologist
Tinton Falls, New Jersey

Sydney Zentall
Professor of Special Education
 and Psychological Sciences
Purdue University
West Lafayette, Indiana

1. Introduction

The responsibility for meeting the educational needs of children with attention deficit disorder (ADD) does not belong to one segment of the education system, but rather to the education system as a whole.

During the reauthorization of the Education for all Handicapped Children Act of 1975 (now renamed the Individuals with Disabilities Education Act [IDEA] of 1990) several members of Congress, at the urging of parent organizations, raised the question of whether or not to add the term *attention deficit disorder* (ADD)* as a separate handicapping condition under Part B of IDEA. A number of educational associations (including CEC) opposed the addition of ADD as a separate category, arguing that (a) children with ADD who require special education may be served under the existing categories of learning disability, serious emotional disturbance, and other health impairment; and (b) the addition of ADD as a category would be counterproductive because of the lack of professional consensus regarding definitional and diagnostic criteria. In addition, there were concerns surrounding the potential overidentification of children who are culturally and linguistically diverse. In response, Congress compromised by requiring the Department of Education to publish a Notice of Inquiry in order to obtain input from the field. In addition, the Department was required to establish four centers to gather and disseminate information pertaining to ADD.

In September 1991, the Department of Education issued a policy clarification on the issue of children with attention deficit disorder. The memorandum, which was jointly signed by the Office of Special Education and Rehabilitative Services, the Office of Civil Rights, and the Office of Elementary and Secondary Education, was intended to clarify state and local responsibility under federal law for meeting the needs of children with ADD in the educational system as a whole. The memo stated that a child with ADD may qualify for special education and related services under Part B of IDEA, through the category of "Other Health Impaired," in instances where "the ADD is a chronic or acute health problem that results in limited alertness, which adversely affects educational performance." Children with ADD are also eligible for services under Part B when they satisfy the criteria applicable to other disability categories such as learning disability, serious emotional disturbance, and so on.

Note: Throughout this booklet, *ADD* will be used to refer to attention deficit disorder, attention deficit hyperactivity disorder (*ADHD*), or attention deficit disorder without hyperactivity.

In addition, even if a child does not qualify for special education and related services under Part B of IDEA, the requirements of Section 504 of the vocational Rehabilitation Act of 1973 (which prohibits discrimination on the basis of disability) may still be applicable. Under Section 504, the school must conduct an evaluation to determine whether or not the child is "handicapped" as defined by the law. If the child is found to have "a physical or mental impairment which substantially limits a major life activity (e.g., learning)," then the local education agency (LEA) must make an "individualized determination of the child's educational needs for regular or special education or related aids or services." As required under Part B, Section 504 also stipulates that the child's education must be provided in the regular classroom, "unless it is demonstrated that education in the regular environment with the use of supplementary aids and services cannot be achieved satisfactorily." According to the memorandum, "through the use of appropriate adaptations and interventions in regular classes, many of which may be required by Section 504, the Department believes that LEAs will be able to effectively address the instructional needs of many children with ADD." Figures 1 and 2 illustrate how the provisions of IDEA and Section 504 are related.

Clearly, the responsibility for meeting the educational needs of children with ADD does not belong to one particular segment of the education system, but rather to the education system as a whole. Thus, if the needs of such children are to be fully met in the schools (whether through general or through special education programs), increased coordination, collaboration and consultation will have to occur among regular educators, special educators, administrators, and related services personnel.

2. CEC Examines the Issues

CEC Task Force addresses three major perspectives that will shape future services: (1) children with ADD are currently in both general and special education programs; (2) these children are at greater risk of developing learning and/or behavioral problems; (3) all teachers and administrators want information on how to meet the needs of these children.

In the summer of 1991, CEC's Committee on Advocacy and Governmental Relations created a Task Force to examine issues surrounding children with ADD in our schools. The purpose of the Task Force was to (a)

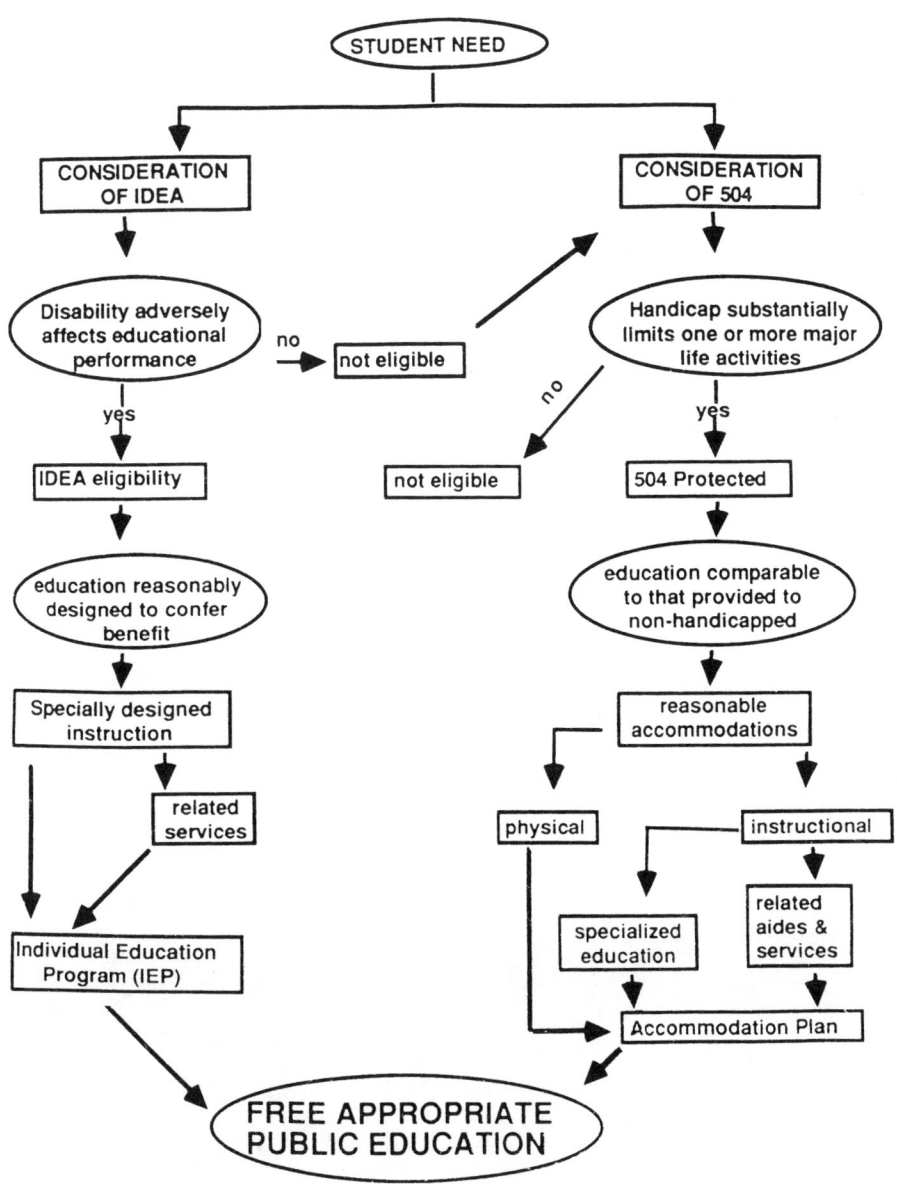

FIGURE 1. IDEA/504 Flow Chart

Reprinted with permission, Council of Administrators of Special Education.

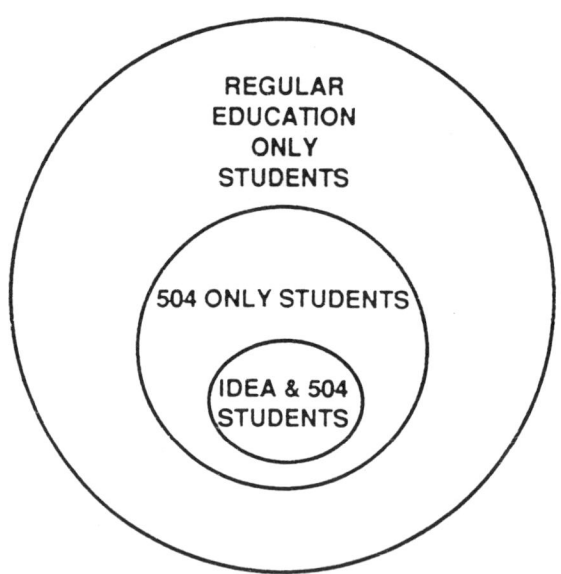

IDEA/504 STUDENTS

Students are qualified under one or more of thirteen (13) IDEA disabling conditions. Specially designed individual education programs are planned for each student by IEP Teams

SECTION 504 STUDENTS ONLY

Due to substantial mental or physical impairments that limit one or more of the student's major life activities, special accommodations to the student's program are required. A 504 accommodation plan is designed for each student according to individual need.
Examples of potential 504 handicapping conditions not typically covered under IDEA are:
-communicable diseases - HIV, Tuberculosis
-medical conditions - asthma, allergies, diabetes, heart disease
-temporary medical conditions due to illness or accident
-Attention Deficit Disorder (ADD, ADHA)
-behavioral difficulties
-drug/alcohol addiction
-other conditions

FIGURE 2. Student Population

Reprinted with permission, Council of Administrators of Special Education.

aggressively explore and develop appropriate interventions in general education programs for children with ADD; (b) recommend ways in which the federal government can provide meaningful support to the entire education community in the provision of educational programming for children with ADD; and (c) continue to develop and communicate CEC's position with respect to children with ADD who may require special education.

The Task Force, a core working group of seven individuals (the majority of whom are school-based personnel) was charged with gathering as much relevant information as possible in order to develop a practical, comprehensive document that could be used (a) to guide CEC policy and (b) as a resource for parents, educators, and others concerned with the education of children with ADD in our schools.

In an effort to have the benefit of a wider range of professional knowledge, the Task Force appointed various individuals (both CEC members and others) with experience and expertise in the area of attention deficit disorder to serve as consultants. In addition to providing written and/or verbal information to the Task Force relating to their area of expertise, the consultants provided the valuable service of critiquing the Task Force report for content, accuracy, and relevance.

The Task Force obtained information for this report through a variety of avenues, which included written and verbal information supplied by the consultants, published sources (books, articles, and research papers), a written survey of parents attending a CH.A.D.D. (Children with Attention Deficit Disorders) conference in Washington, DC, and a public hearing.

The hearing, conducted during CEC's Conference on At-Risk Children in November 1991, enabled the Task Force to hear testimony presented by parents, educators, researchers, and related services personnel. The Task Force asked witnesses to address one or more of the following issues: successful intervention strategies in special and general education classrooms; appropriate administrative and programmatic options for better meeting the educational needs of children with ADD; options for other children with diverse learning needs; issues surrounding diagnosis and assessment; information regarding children who are culturally and linguistically diverse; and teacher training across the education profession.

In the course of gathering information regarding ADD, the following overriding issues quickly emerged:

1. Regardless of how ADD is defined or diagnosed, children exhibiting the characteristics of ADD are currently in our classrooms, in both general and special education programs.

2. Such children may have (or are at greater risk of developing) learning and behavioral problems associated with ADD.
3. School-based personnel (both general and special education teachers and administrators) want and need information on how best to meet the needs of such children. In particular, educators want information on how to provide support to children with the characteristics of ADD before these characteristics cause such children to fall into a rapidly accelerating downward spiral of academic and social failure.

It is hoped that this resource will be used by educators and parents in their struggle to adequately meet the educational needs of children with the characteristics of ADD. Additional information on appropriate interventions and diagnostic techniques should be made available through the federally funded Centers on ADD beginning in early 1993. These centers are listed in the Additional Resources section at the back of this booklet.

The recommendations and interventions listed in this booklet are not necessarily the "best" practices, nor are they intended to represent the full range of interventions and practices currently being used with children with ADD in our schools today. However, the booklet reflects the thoughts and advice of parents, professionals, and leaders from the field of special education regarding what they believe to be appropriate components of effective school programs for children with ADD. It is hoped that school-based personnel will use this booklet as a starting point in their efforts to better meet the needs of children with ADD in their particular schools.

In addition, although the information provided here focuses on children with the characteristics of ADD, many of the interventions and strategies may be useful for other children who are experiencing educational difficulties that place them at greater risk for school failure.

3. Prevalence and Characteristics of Attention Deficit Disorder

Between 1.35 and 2.25 million school-age children in the United States may have an attention deficit disorder. Characteristics include developmentally inappropriate degrees of inattention, impulsiveness, and/or hyperactivity.

Many experts estimate that children with ADD constitute 3% to 5% of the current school-age population, which would represent 1.35 to 2.25

million children. According to the Professional Group for ADD and Related Disorders (PGARD), in their comments to the Department of Education's Notice of Inquiry (1991), approximately 50% of children with ADD do not require special education services, but rather "appropriate recognition or modifications to the regular program of instruction." PGARD estimates that of the 50% who do require special education, about 85% are able to receive a significant proportion of their instruction in the regular classroom. Recent evidence indicates that about one-third of the children identified as having a specific learning disability also have an attention deficit disorder, and that anywhere from 30% to 65% of children identified as having serious emotional disturbance also have attention deficit disorder.

According to the Virginia Department of Education's Task Force report (1990), "the condition which today is termed 'Attention Deficit Hyperactivity Disorder' (ADHD) has been recognized as an entity for at least the last half century." Children with the characteristics of ADD were, at different points, described as "brain injured," "hyperactive," or thought to have "minimal brain dysfunction." Currently, the *Diagnostic and Statistical Manual of Mental Disorders, Third Edition–Revised* (DSM-III-R, 1987) characterizes ADD as "developmentally inappropriate degrees of inattention, impulsiveness, and hyperactivity." Although hyperactivity is more common among younger children, other ADD characteristics may persist into adulthood. The DSM-III-R lists 14 behaviors thought to be prevalent among children with ADD, and it specifies that the child must exhibit, prior to age 7, at least 8 of the 14 behaviors at a greater frequency than observed among others of the same mental age. In addition, the characteristics must have been present for at least 6 months. The behaviors are as follows:

1. often fidgets with hands or feet or squirms in seat (in adolescents, may be limited to subjective feeling of restlessness);

2. has difficulty remaining seated when required to do so;

3. is easily distracted by extraneous stimuli;

4. has difficulty awaiting turn in games or group situations;

5. often blurts out answers to questions before they have been completed;

6. has difficulty following through on instructions from others (not due to oppositional behavior or failure of comprehension); e.g., fails to finish chores;

7. has difficulty sustaining attention in tasks or play activities;

8. often shifts from one uncompleted activity to another;

9. has difficulty playing quietly;
10. often talks excessively;
11. often interrupts or intrudes on others, e.g., butts into other children's games;
12. often does not seem to listen to what is being said to him or her;
13. often loses things necessary for tasks or activities at school or at home (e.g., toys, pencils, books, assignments); and/or
14. often engages in physically dangerous activities without considering possible consequences (not for the purpose of thrill-seeking); e.g., runs into street without looking. (pp. 52-53)

Based on the frequency and intensity of the above behaviors, the child's disorder can be classified as mild, moderate, or severe. In 1993, another classification formulation (DSM-IV) is expected to be published, which may include changes in the operational diagnostic criteria.

Another description of ADD that may be useful for educators was contained in PGARD's (1991) response to the Notice of Inquiry:

> The condition "attention deficit disorder" refers to a developmental disorder involving one or more of the basic cognitive processes related to orienting, focusing or maintaining attention, resulting in a marked degree of inadequate attention to academic and social tasks. The disorder may also include verbal or motor impulsivity and excessive nontask related activities such as fidgeting or restlessness. The inattentive behavior of ADD most commonly has onset in early childhood, remains inappropriate for age, and persists throughout development. (p. 2)

In terms of educational impact, the ADD may "adversely affect educational performance to the extent that a significant discrepancy exists between a child's intellectual ability and that child's educational productivity with respect to listening, following directions, planning, organizing or completing academic assignments that require reading, writing, spelling or mathematical calculations" (PGARD, 1991, p. 2).

According to Zentall (1991b), in her testimony before the Task Force, "what is easy to recognize and therefore salient in the early identification of ADHD youth is increased verbal and motoric activity. What characterizes this activity is not only its intensity (loudness, frequency) but the fact that it is highly variable in nature (i.e., very different from the repetitive activity and ideation that characterizes anxious and autistic individuals)" (p. 2).

Other characteristics frequently seen in children with ADD are temper outbursts, low self-esteem, and variable mood (Reeve, 1990). Boys tend to be diagnosed four to nine times as often as girls, and, when compared to girls with ADD, are more aggressive, impulsive, and destructive. Because they tend to be underidentified and thus underserved, girls with ADD may be at risk for long-term academic, social, and emotional difficulties (Parker, 1992).

A child may not exhibit behaviors associated with ADD in some situations (i.e., in novel situations, or those in which the child is receiving considerable attention or has chosen the activity). However, the ADD behaviors are almost always present under conditions in which the child is engaged in a boring or difficult task that requires attention for an extended period and is without direct supervision (Reeve, personal communication, May 1992).

DSM-III-R also contains a second diagnostic category, "undifferentiated attention deficit disorder" (UADD), which refers to children who display significant inattentiveness, but without hyperactivity. Such children are generally not impulsive, and they tend to be underactive rather than overactive. Teachers tend to describe children with UADD as daydreamers, confused, and lethargic. Studies indicate that children with UADD are at high risk for academic failure, and they may have a higher rate of associated learning problems than children with ADD who are also hyperactive (Parker, 1992).

Most experts agree that ADD is a neurobiological disorder that can have multiple causes. Heredity appears to play a role, as research indicates that children with ADD are likely to have a biological relative with ADD. In addition, evidence suggests that neurological, neurochemical, or, in some cases, toxic factors may be involved. Other factors such as other medical conditions, medication side effects, familial functioning, or environmental conditions may exacerbate an existing disorder or contribute to the development of ADD-like problems in some children (Parker, 1992).

4. Evaluation

A two-tiered process of evaluation is recommended (1) to determine whether or not a child meets the criteria for diagnosis of ADD and (2) to determine the degree to which the child's educational performance is adversely affected.

As with all other disabling conditions, evaluation methods for children suspected of having ADD should be a multistep, multidisciplinary procedure. In their response to the Department of Education's Notice of

Inquiry, PGARD recommends using a two-tiered process for evaluating a child suspected of having ADD. Tier 1 of the assessment should determine whether the child meets the criteria for diagnosis of ADD. If the tier 1 assessment confirms the presence of ADD, then a tier 2 evaluation would be required. Tier 2 of the assessment should determine the degree to which the child's educational performance is adversely affected. Tier 2 assessments will help determine what types of educational services are necessary to assist the student.

Diagnosing ADD (tier 1) requires gathering information about the child from a number of sources and in a variety of ways. Medical information; parent or guardian descriptions of the child's physical, mental, social, and emotional development; school information; descriptions of social behavior and classroom adjustment; and assessment of the child's cognitive functioning are essential to making a diagnosis. Evaluation methods for children suspected of having ADD often include the use of rating scales for parents and teachers. Because the behavior of children thought to have ADD can vary widely in different situations and environments, experts recommend obtaining information from a wide variety of sources and observing the child in a variety of settings and at different time periods.

If the tier 1 diagnostic evaluation results in a diagnosis of ADD, then the tier 2 evaluation should be done to determine to what extent the child's ADD affects his or her academic performance. For a number of reasons, school personnel play an important role in collecting data for this stage of the assessment. Teachers may be best able to document the degree of impairment of academic performance the child exhibits in class. This can be done through direct observation, teacher-completed academic performance rating scales, sampling of roll-book grades or work samples collected over a specified period of time, or via the results of trial interventions implemented by the teacher under the direction of the child study team or a teacher assistant team.

Popper (1991) has recommended that a child suspected of having ADD be carefully evaluated to rule out the possibility that the child has a "look-alike" disorder. According to Popper, "Look-alike ADD children may fulfill the diagnostic criteria for ADD but have a completely different problem and, therefore, should receive a different diagnosis. These ADD look-alikes are important to distinguish because their long-term treatment may be quite different from children with classical ADD" (p. 16). The disorders that can result in ADD-like characteristics include depression, stress-induced anxiety states, biologically based anxiety disorders, child abuse or neglect, bipolar disorders, schizophrenia, or other medical disorders (such as sleep disorders, malfunctions of the thyroid gland, or excessive lead ingestion). Popper has advised that numerous problems must be contemplated, assessed, and ruled out before a diagnosis of ADD can be made.

In addition, individuals with expertise in the education of children who are culturally and linguistically diverse caution that many of the characteristics in the DSM-III-R list may be attributable to cultural or linguistic differences in the child. In her testimony before the Task Force, Ortiz (1991) pointed out that

> As many as 10 out of 14 of the behaviors typically associated with ADD are typical of students who are acquiring a second language. Normally a child who is limited English proficient and who is being taught in English will have difficulty following instructions; may appear not to be listening; may be easily distracted by extraneous stimuli; will have difficulty sustaining attention on tasks; and will often times shift from one uncompleted activity to another. These and other types of behavior typically associated with ADD (e.g., being socially withdrawn, nervous and anxious; poor school performance; poor self concept; poor academic motivation) could be exhibited by students in the process of acquiring a second language.

Thus, the importance of obtaining information from a variety of sources (i.e., parents, teachers, etc.) when evaluating a child is underscored.

In order to avoid the inappropriate referral of children who are linguistically and culturally diverse, experts such as the National Association of Black Psychologists and PGARD recommend that when conducting an evaluation of such a child, at least one member of the evaluation team (a) be a member of the same (or a similar) ethnic, cultural, or linguistic minority group; or (b) have expertise in the evaluation of children who are members of that minority group. PGARD also recommends that rating scales and other assessment instruments be used in the context of the norms for the minority group of which the child is a member.

5. Prereferral Intervention and Teacher Assistance Teams

Proactive strategies, such as prereferral intervention and the use of teacher assistance teams, help to reduce the risk of underachievement and academic and social failure.

As was mentioned in the introduction, children diagnosed with attention deficit disorder may qualify for special education and related services under the category of "other health impaired," as well as under other categories for which they meet the established criteria. However, in order to be eligible for services under *any* category under IDEA, the disability must have an adverse impact on the child's educational performance. Similarly, a child's disability must "substantially limit" one or more major life activities (e.g., learning) in order for the child to be eligible for services under Section 504 of the Vocational Rehabilitation Act. Thus, in many instances, children who are experiencing educational difficulties, whether stemming from ADD or some other cause, often fail to receive any assistance until *after* their difficulties (i.e., distractibility, disorganization, inability to complete assignments on time, etc.) have caused them to fall significantly behind their classmates. Unfortunately, by the time children have experienced such failure they have already lost a great deal of academic ground. In addition, school failure may contribute to or worsen a student's feelings of low self-esteem, depression, or anxiety.

In order to prevent such negative consequences, many experts recommend the use of proactive approaches such as prereferral interventions. Broadly defined, a prereferral intervention is a systematic and collaborative effort to assist regular education teachers in using interventions with hard-to-teach students (Parker, 1992). In this model, the design and application of interventions is done through a team approach. Such teams (e.g., child study teams, child study committees, teacher assistance teams) often consist of the regular education teacher, a school psychologist or counselor, and a special educator, but they can include experts in the area of ADD, teachers of children with emotional or behavioral disorders, physicians, the school nurse, social workers, and others. The team assists the teacher in assessing the student's behavior and implementing systematic modification programs until the student's problems are corrected or until it is decided that more intensive intervention is necessary.

For example, a student suspected of having ADD may be brought to the child study team by a teacher who is looking for ways to help the child. The team might suggest that the child receive a formal ADD screening and a more complete evaluation for ADD if the screening evaluation suggests so. In conjunction with the screening or full evaluation results, team members might make various recommendations to the teacher regarding accommodations the teacher could use with the student in the classroom. In addition, the team might help the teacher design and implement a formal behavior management program for the student. If difficulties at home are suspected, a social worker or family counselor may be consulted. Other recommendations may include enrolling the child in a social skills program, or assigning a case manager to follow up and stay in contact with the teacher. A flow chart of the prereferral procedures recommended for children suspected of having ADD by a

Superintendent's Task Force in Broward County, Florida, is shown in Figure 3.

Initiating proactive, or preventive, interventions may reduce the child's risk of underachievement and academic and social failure. However, if such preventive strategies are insufficient to maintain or improve the child's educational performance, then the team should consider referral for additional programs and services.

Another example of a proactive approach is the Teacher Assistance Team model described by Chalfant, Pysh, and Moultrie (1979). According to this approach, teachers who have students who are having difficulties request assistance from teams of colleagues. A team meets with a teacher in a 30-minute problem-solving session to discuss the problem and design an intervention plan, which the teacher then implements with the help of the team. Faculty of the University of Texas at Austin, who have been using this method in a school district with a 70% Hispanic enrollment, have resolved, on average, 70% of the cases considered without referral to special education (Ortiz, 1991). In addition to leading to better identification of children who may have disabilities, this method provides data—through an analysis of teacher requests for assistance—that can be used to design comprehensive inservice programs for building-based professional development activities.

Clearly, proactive approaches are also crucial to the effort of reducing the numbers of children who are culturally and linguistically diverse being referred inappropriately to special education programs. Prereferral interventions provide teachers with problem-solving strategies other than referral to special education when students are exhibiting educational difficulties. Thus, students who are experiencing difficulty because of limited English proficiency or because of socioeconomic or other factors unrelated to having a disability would be more likely to receive the support they need in the regular classroom without being unnecessarily (and incorrectly) identified as having a disability.

6. Multidisciplinary Approaches and Professional Collaboration

Effective programs use a multidisciplinary approach to meeting the needs of children with ADD and encourage professional collaboration.

Collaborative and multidisciplinary approaches are an integral component of any proactive strategy for meeting the needs of children with ADD, just as they are for dealing with other children experiencing

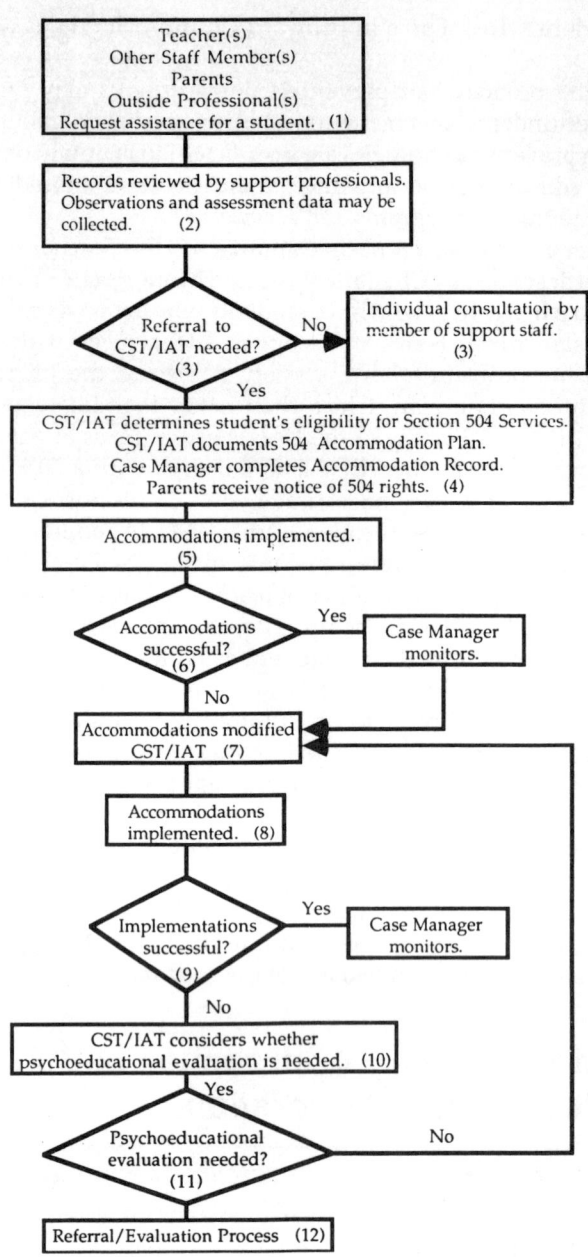

FIGURE 3. Flow Chart for Students with Attention Deficit Problems and Those with other Handicapping Conditions
Source: *Superintendent's Task Force Report on Attention Deficit Disorder, 1991.* Broward County Public Schools, Student Services, Broward County, Florida.

(1) The student referral is directed to the school designee* (counselor, administrators, etc.).

(2) Available records are reviewed by selected support professionals (e.g., school psychologist, counselor, social worker, etc.). Observations may be conducted and other pertinent data collected at this time.

(3) Selected support team members, e.g., school psychologist, counselor, social worker, etc.) will review the student's records and additional data in order to determine if there is a need for the Child Study Team/Intervention Assistance Team (CST/IAT) to review the case. At this point a referral could be considered to the CST/IAT.

(4) The CST/IAT reviews the student's records and determines if the student meets the classification as a qualified handicapped individual under Section 504 of the Rehabilitation Act of 1973.

If the student is considered a candidate for 504 services, the teacher(s), parents, and support professionals collaborate in planning accommodation strategies. These accommodations are documented on a 504 Accommodation Plan. Finally a case manager is assigned from the school staff (e.g., school designee, counselor, administration, team leader, etc.) to monitor the student's progress. The case manager is responsible for completing the 504 Accommodation Record form and setting timeliness for implementing and monitoring the accommodations.

Parents receive copies of the 504 Accommodation Plan and 504 Accommodation Record forms, along with a formal notice of the rights afforded to them by Section 504 of the Rehabilitation Act of 1973.

(5) Teacher, parent, and support professionals will participate directly in implementing the accommodations. Support professionals remain accessible to the teacher/parent and offer additional suggestions as necessary.

(6) The effectiveness of accommodations is evaluated by the assigned case manager from the school staff (e.g., school designee, counselor, administrator, team leader, etc.). If the accommodations need to be modified or redesigned, the case is resubmitted to the CST/IAT.

(7), (8), (9) See (4), (5), and (6).

(10) If the accommodations have proven ineffective, the CST/IAT will consider referring the student for a psychoeducational evaluation.

(11) and (12) The case will be handled by the ESE Specialist if the psychoeducational evaluation is recommended. If the pyschoeducational evaluation is not recommended, the CST/IAT will continue revising its intervention plan.

*School designee is assigned by the principal.

FIGURE 3. (Continued)

educational difficulties (whether caused by a disability or other mitigating factors). As previously mentioned, the characteristics of ADD may, depending on their nature and severity, result in learning, social, emotional and/or behavioral difficulties for the student. Appropriate interventions may include instructional or curricular modifications, changes in the classroom environment, behavioral and/or cognitive modification strategies, and/or medical interventions. The support of related services personnel in providing any of these above interventions (or any combination thereof) can be crucial to their successful implementation. Professionals such as the school nurse, social worker, school psychologist, and other appropriate pupil services personnel should be made available to provide direct and/or consultative services as needed. In addition, special education professionals should, as appropriate, provide advice and guidance to the regular classroom teacher. They can be particularly helpful in designing individualized instructional approaches.

An example of another collaborative (and proactive) approach designed to provide support to children with diverse learning needs in the regular classroom is the Creative, Useful, Experiential Learning Program being implemented in the Coloma Community Schools, Michigan. In this program, all children remain in regular classrooms while specialty teachers move from room to room, working with students as needed. This program provides teachers and other professionals with the flexibility to work together to develop coursework appropriate to the needs of a particular child. According to Mary Spessard (1992), who directs the program, educational outcomes for special education students have improved under this system, while referrals to special education have decreased by nearly 50%.

The role of administrators and school leaders is important to the implementation of collaborative, or teaming approaches. According to Villa and Thousand (1990), building- and district-level administrators can play a number of vital roles in a team-based model, including the following:

- Modifying master schedules to support teachers with the time needed to meet as teams.
- Creating job descriptions that reflect the new roles of professionals working in a team-based system.
- Hiring personnel who embrace the district's philosophy and have appropriate technical and communication skills.
- Supervising and evaluating staff in a manner that supports the district's commitment to all children.

- Setting the agenda for staff meetings and including items that relate to the support needs of all children.
- Arranging for inservice and training for staff.

7. Communication

Effective programs encourage frequent parent-professional and professional-professional communication.

The parents who responded to the Task Force survey described a wide variety of educational interventions that had been effective with their children. Although the survey failed to reveal any one typical program or intervention, one common factor did emerge: Programs described as effective by the parents in meeting the needs of their child all communicated frequently and effectively with the parents, usually via phone calls, notebooks, or regular meetings. Parents described their frustration with schools that failed to notify them of their child's progress until the child had fallen irretrievably behind. One parent wrote that "what would have helped was phone calls at the first sign of trouble. I could have hopped on the problem immediately.... Our school notified us on a report card 2 months later that as many as 17 assignments were missed. Needless to say my child never recovered and the rest of the year was worth very little."

Current research indicates that parental involvement is important in improving the educational outcomes for *all* children. For children with ADD (or any other disability or factor causing educational difficulty), such involvement is even more crucial. The child's parents can provide the teacher with information regarding the child's strengths, needs, and interests. In addition, parents can work with the teacher to reinforce at home the organizational skills and strategies that are so crucial to success in the classroom. Several parents described programs in which they would cooperate with the teacher to provide special rewards at home for appropriate school achievement or behavior.

Education professionals may need to recognize, however, that not all parents may be able (or willing) to become so actively involved with their child's education. In addition to the stressors facing many families (e.g., juggling career/family responsibilities, single parent households, economic difficulties, etc.), the parents of children with ADD face the additional demands of parenting a child who may need a great deal of care and supervision (Parker, 1992). However, regardless of how active or involved parents may choose to be in their child's education, school personnel should make every effort to maintain open lines of communication and keep parents informed of the child's progress.

Many parents who responded to the Task Force survey indicated that receiving good communication from the child's school depended, from year to year, on the particular teacher. Several parents mentioned that their schools discouraged parental involvement, and never initiated communication. The importance of effective professional collaboration and communication between professionals and parents should be stressed in both professional preparation and continuing education programs for administrators and teachers.

Because children with ADD may require the services of other professionals (e.g., medical, counseling, social work, etc.), it is important that the school have an established procedure for frequent communication with such personnel (and relevant agencies) in order to provide better coordination of services. Communication between physicians and the schools is especially important in instances in which the child is receiving medication for his or her ADD. As Parker has pointed out in *The ADD Hyperactivity Handbook for Schools* (1992), "Schools play an ever increasing role in the monitoring of medication effects on children. For most children, the primary effects of medication will only be noticeable during school hours, so teachers will be very important informants as to how well the medication works and how well the child tolerates it." An example of a medication checklist for school personnel is shown in Figure 4.

In many instances, the school nurse or other school professional such as a social worker can often play a vital role as a liaison between the agencies or professionals who are providing services to the child, as well as to the parents.

8. Positive School Climate

Effective programs create a positive school climate and provide the support, flexibility, and continuing education needed by teachers to meet diverse educational needs.

Several witnesses who testified at the Task Force hearing described the importance of a positive school climate in meeting the educational needs of children with the characteristics of ADD. According to Eleanor Guetzloe (1991), Professor of Special Education at the University of South Florida, a positive school climate will be attained through the provision of physical safety, psychological security, attainable goals, relevant curriculum, effective instruction, charismatic staff, avoidance of punishment, opportunities for socialization, and an atmosphere of

MEDICATION EFFECTS RATING SCALE

Name _____ Completed by _____
Date of Birth _____ Age _____ Sex _____ Grade _____
Date form completed _____

Medication(s)   Dosages and Times Administered Per Day

_____ _____

Mark any changes in the following behaviors:

Main Effects on Behavior	Worse	No Difference	Improved a Little	Improved a Lot
Attention to task				
Listening to lessons				
Finishing assigned work				
Impulsivity				
Calling out in class				
Organizing work				
Overactivity				
Restless, fidgety				
Talkative				
Aggressive				
Peer interaction				

Mark any side effects which you have noticed or which the child has mentioned.

	Side Effects	Comments
_____	Appetite loss	_____
_____	Insomnia	_____
_____	Headaches	_____
_____	Stomachaches	_____
_____	Seems tired	_____
_____	Stares a lot	_____
_____	Irritability	_____
_____	Excessive crying	_____
_____	Motor/vocal tic	_____
_____	Nervousness	_____
_____	Sadness	_____
_____	Withdrawn	_____

FIGURE 4. Medication Effects Rating Scale

Source: *The ADD Hyperactivity Handbook for Schools* by Harvey C. Parker. (800) ADD-WARE. Reprinted with permission. This form may be reproduced for classroom use.

caring. In addition, the child should be given a clean slate every day; that is, each day should provide a new opportunity to succeed, free and clear of yesterday's failures.

In such a positive climate, the teacher should have the knowledge and skills necessary to be aware of the need for changes in the curriculum to meet individual needs, including dividing up long tasks into shorter ones; providing breaks; creating appropriate physical conditions; and using flexibility in giving assignments, scheduling, and grading. In addition, the teacher should provide appropriate consequences for a child's behavior (i.e., rather than punishing the child for hyperactive behavior, the teacher should provide the child with appropriate ways to channel his or her high activity level).

Many parents mentioned the importance of having a caring, nonjudgmental, and supportive teacher in the creation of a positive educational atmosphere for their children. One parent stated that "the teacher must be positive and believe in the child's ability rather than disability." Another noted that "positive attitudes and communication from the teacher that he is liked and accepted" are very important in motivating her child. Another parent mentioned that the key to her child's success is a "supportive, encouraging teacher who makes it clear that she values the child first and then will deal with any behavior problems, rather than conveying to our son that he's a 'bad' or 'problem' kid."

The Task Force recognizes that many schools have not come close to providing positive climates for children *or* teachers due to financial concerns, the lack of adequate facilities, and shortages of qualified personnel. Positive school climates are most easily created, of course, in environments that provide teachers with the resources and education necessary to do their jobs adequately. However, even without the infusion of funds or other drastic changes, modifications and/or the flexible use of existing programs and resources can often result in positive changes for both children and teachers. In all schools, teachers can and should be provided with the support, advice, and assistance of other education professionals as necessary. In addition, school leaders, administrators, and other professionals must be fully committed to and involved in the process of providing appropriate educational services to children with diverse learning needs in the regular classroom. As previously mentioned, the support of administrators and school leaders is crucial. They have the authority to allocate resources, provide educators with the time necessary to collaborate or meet as teams, and provide the necessary continuing education for staff.

Teachers must not be faced with the prospect of referring all children who are exhibiting educational difficulties to special education as the only means of obtaining additional support services.

9. Continuing Education and Staff Development

Effective programs provide the continuing education and staff development necessary for successful program implementation.

Many parents, as well as professionals, believe that the key to creating positive climates lies in improved professional preparation and staff development for both teachers and administrators. According to Fowler (1991), "Effectively educating children with ADD begins when both parents and educators fully understand the disability and its potential for adversely affecting educational performance, whether that performance is academic, social or both" (p. 2).

Effective professional preparation and staff development programs for the training of educators will help teachers develop realistic social and academic expectations for the child. In addition, improved knowledge will help reduce inappropriate punishment of children for "noncompliance," when these children have great difficulty complying as a result of having ADD. Such inappropriate punishment for ADD related behaviors are ineffective in improving a child's performance, and they only prove frustrating for both student and teacher.

Effective staff education programs for both regular and special education professionals is also crucial to the success of programs that use collaborative strategies. For example, in the Creative, Useful, Experiential Learning Program described earlier, regular and special education professionals were provided with extensive inservice training prior to program implementation. Teachers and school leaders need to have the skills necessary to recognize diversity in students and to work with other professionals as necessary to provide the student with the particular support he or she needs to learn.

As previously mentioned, professional preparation and continuing education are important in improving services provided to children who are culturally and linguistically diverse. According to Ortiz (1991), "Research at the University of Texas at Austin suggests that neither the data gathered as part of the referral process nor the evaluation decisions made using that data reflects that professionals adequately understand linguistic and cultural differences, socioeconomic status, and other characteristics that mediate students' learning." In order to avoid the inappropriate referral of children who are culturally diverse, Ortiz recommends improved training for educators, particularly those who are serving minority students. In essence, educators must be able "to distinguish when performance is related to linguistic and cultural differences versus when behaviors suggest the presence of an attention deficit disorder."

Ortiz has further advised that teachers be prepared in areas such as basic concepts regarding language differences; including second language learning and dialectal differences; frameworks for observing and interpreting cultural characteristics; the provision of instruction that is linguistically and culturally relevant; and the provision of instruction that focuses on higher order thinking in problem-solving and learning strategies. In addition, given that demographic data indicate that classrooms will have larger and larger numbers of students who reflect diversity in terms of language, culture, socioeconomic status, and learning style, both regular and special education professionals should have training in the management of diversity in today's classroom.

10. Classroom Strategies That Help Children Focus on Learning Tasks

Effective strategies include seating the student near the teacher; shortening or reducing the difficulty of assignments; teaching learning strategies; using behavioral approaches; teaching social skills; and providing assistance in learning how to organize.

Appropriate strategies for meeting the educational needs of a child with ADD will differ from child to child, since, as Forness and Walker (1991) have pointed out, "the problems of any individual child with this diagnosis may vary considerably depending on age, presence or absence of associated problems, level of academic performance, and a variety of other factors related to school functioning" (p. 2). However, certain instructional strategies and classroom modifications have been found to be useful in the education of children with ADD. According to Ortiz (1991), such strategies can also be "very effective with minority children, if they are delivered in ways that reflect the understanding of language and culture."

Forness and Walker have recommended the following strategies:

- Seat the student close to the teacher so that the child can hear and see what is being asked or demonstrated and the teacher in turn can monitor the student's progress and be more readily available if help is needed. If the classroom has an aide or adult volunteer, it may in some cases be more useful to seat the student where this person can assist the child without undue interruption to the class. (1991c)

- Shorten or reduce the difficulty of the assignment for an individual student so that she or he has the sense of completing the task in the same length of time as other students. The teacher or aide may need to modify, monitor, or reduce only those lessons in which the child has particular trouble.

- Provide instruction in *learning strategies*. Children with ADD frequently have great difficulty in monitoring and regulating their behavior to fit the changing demands of both school and social situations. Children with ADD often seem unable to employ learning strategies that other children generate routinely (i.e., talking themselves silently through new tasks until the tasks become automatic). The following approach can be used to teach such strategies to children with ADD: (a) isolating techniques that may be necessary for certain tasks; (b) demonstrating or modeling them for the child; (c) having the child rehearse the strategies; (d) providing the child with feedback; and (e) encouraging and monitoring the child the first few times he or she uses the strategy in actual practice. (1991a)

    It may be necessary to cue the child as to when to use the strategy on new but similar tasks and even to instruct the child on which strategies should be used with which sets of tasks or lessons. The overall goal is to diminish the child's reliance on these external prompts and cues and eventually to have these strategies become as automatic as possible. (1991a)

    Other approaches in this general area of strategy instruction may involve self-monitoring or self-recording of the child's own behaviors, such as off- and on-task behaviors during a given period. Self-organizing skills are another form of strategy training in which the child is systematically taught approaches to certain tasks. For example, for homework, the student could be taught to: (a) find a quiet place at home to work; (b) break assignments into smaller parts (if there is a page or more of problems to do, divide the assignment into 3 or 4 parts); (c) spend 10 or 15 minutes on each section (keep a clock or timer nearby to keep track of time); (d) stop working when time is up or the section is completed; and (e) take a break before using the same procedure with the next section of work. (1991a)

- Use behavioral approaches. Among the more common approaches are the use of checks or points that are awarded to the child for specific behaviors or accomplishments. For very young children, stars or stickers may be used. The checks or stickers can be exchanged periodically in the classroom for a few minutes of free time or an enjoyable activity or else saved up over a longer period (i.e., the end of each day or a week) for a special activity. For some students, providing verbal praise for appropriate behaviors and ignoring unwanted or off-task behaviors is very effective. (1991a)

- Provide social skills instruction. While most children develop social skills by observing and interacting with others, the child with ADD may not profit as readily from these interactions or may have diminished opportunity to learn because of social rejection. A number of commercially available social skills instructional programs are now becoming available for use by teachers. Some of these curricula are designed to cover instruction systematically over a period of time on a variety of topics, such as basic manners, asking for help, asking for permission, beginning and carrying on a conversation, initiating an activity, and sharing belongings. (1991b)

- Provide organizational assistance. Students may need to be taught how to organize their lessons and assignments, taking advantage of notebook dividers, notebooks that have specific pockets for pencils and other materials, and notebooks that zip shut. Desk trays or labeled boxes to help store materials in specific places and periodic daily checks of desks to see that all materials are stored correctly may also be helpful. An extra set of books from the school may be requested for home use so that there are no excuses for losing books or not being able to complete homework assignments. (1991a)

11. Classroom Strategies That Accommodate Different Abilities to Maintain Attention and Keep Activity Within Certain Levels

Appropriate school behavior and learning are dependent on a child's ability to orient, maintain attention, and keep activity within certain levels for extended periods of time.

Zentall (1991b), in her testimony before the Task Force, recommended classroom modifications and strategies that recognize the ADD child's need for increased stimulation and capitalize on the positive aspects of the child's behavioral and learning characteristics. The following material is a summary of her recommendations:

Principles of Remediation for Excessive Activity

- Do not attempt to reduce activity, but channel it into acceptable avenues.
  a. Encourage directed movement in classrooms that is not disruptive.
  b. Allow standing during seatwork, especially near the end of the task.
- Use activity as reward.
  a. Give permission for an activity (e.g., run errand, clean board, organize teacher's desk, arrange chairs) as an individual reward for improvement.
- Use active responses in instruction.
  a. Use teaching activities that encourage active responding (e.g., talking, moving, organizing, working at the board).
  b. Encourage diary writing, painting, and so on.
  c. Teach child to ask questions that are on topic.

Principles of Remediation for Inability to Wait (Impulsivity)

- Do not ask the child to wait, but do give the child substitute verbal or motor responses to make while waiting, and, where possible, do encourage daydreaming or planning in the interim.
  a. Instruct the child on how to continue on easier parts of tasks (or do a substitute task) while waiting for the teacher's help.
  b. Teach the child how to cross out incorrect answers on multiple-choice tests.
  c. Have the child underline or rewrite directions before beginning, or provide colored markers or colored pencils for the child to underline directions or relevant information.
  d. Encourage the child to doodle or play with clay, paperclips, or pipe cleaners while waiting or listening to instructions.
  e. Encourage notetaking (even just cue words).
- When an inability to wait becomes impatience and bossiness, encourage leadership but do not assume that impulsive statements or behavior are aggressive in intent.

a. Suggest and reinforce alternate ways (e.g., line leader, paper passer).
   b. For children who interrupt, teach them to recognize pauses in conversations and how to hang onto ideas.
   c. Cue child about upcoming difficult times or tasks in which extra control will be needed.
   d. Instruct and reinforce social routines (e.g., hello, goodbye, please, thank you).

Principles of Remediation for Failure to Sustain Attention to Routine Tasks and Activities

- Decrease the length of the task.
   a. Break one task into smaller parts to be completed at different times.
   b. Give two tasks, with a preferred task to be completed after the less preferred task.
   c. Give fewer spelling words and mathematics problems.
   d. Use fewer words in explaining tasks (i.e., give concise and global verbal directions).
   e. Use distributed practice rather than massed practice for rote tasks.
- Make tasks interesting.
   a. Allow work with partners, in small groups, and in centers.
   b. Alternate high- and low-interest tasks.
   c. Use an overhead projector when lecturing.
   d. Allow the child to sit closer to the teacher.
- Increase novelty, especially in the later time periods of longer tasks.
   a. Make a game out of checking work.
   b. Use games to overlearn rote material.
- Do not teach or reinforce "dead-man's behavior"; that is, do not assume that the child is not paying attention just because he or she looks out the window or at another child. Do not make on-task behavior a goal without changing the nature of the task or the learning environment.

Principles of Remediation for Noncompliance and Failure to Complete Tasks

- Generally increase the choice and specific interest of tasks for the child.
    a. Allow a limited choice of tasks, topics, and activities.
    b. Determine the child's preferred activities and use them as incentives.
    c. Bring the child's interests into assignments.
- Make sure that the tasks fit within the child's learning abilities and preferred response style.
    a. Allow alternate response modes (e.g., typewriter, computer, taped assignments).
    b. Alter the difficulty level of assignments. (Give advanced-level assignments or lower the level of difficulty.)
    c. Make sure that disorganization is not responsible for failure to complete tasks.

Principles of Remediation for Difficulty at the Beginning of Tasks

- Generally increase the structure and salience of the relevant parts of tasks and social settings.
    a. Prompt the child for verbal directions (e.g., use written directions in addition to verbal ones; encourage notetaking).
    b. Structure written assignments and tests (e.g., use graph paper for math; state standards of acceptable work, being as specific as possible).
    c. Point out the overall structure of tasks (e.g., topic sentences, headings, tables of content).
    d. Allow work with partners or in small groups with quiet talking.
    e. Color, circle, underline, or rewrite directions, difficult letters in spelling, and math process signs.

Principles of Remediation for Completing Assignments on Time

- Increase the use of lists and assignment organizers such as notebooks and folders).
  a. Write assignments for the child in a pocket notebook.
  b. Write assignments on the board and make sure child has copied them.

- Establish object-placement routines to retrieve routinely used objects such as books, assignments, and clothes.
  a. Encourage the use of pocket folders with new work on one side and completed, graded work and class notes organized chronologically on the other.
  b. Encourage parents to establish places for certain things at home (e.g., books, homework).
  c. Help the child organize his or her desk or locker with labels and places for certain items.

- Use color and physical/spatial organizers.
  a. Teach the child the routine of self-questioning before leaving one place for another (e.g., walking out of a door). ("Do I have everything I need?")
  b. Tape prompt cards in desks, on books, or on assignment folders.

Increasing Planning and Sequential Organization of Thought

- Practice planning.
  a. Practice planning different activities (what is needed, how to break tasks into parts).
  b. Practice estimating time needed for activities.
  c. Teach outlining skills.

- Practice sorting, ordering, and reordering.
  a. Teach the use of a word processor to reorder ideas.
  b. Teach the child to take notes on lectures or on written materials in three columns (main points, supporting points, questions).

Principles of Remediation for Poor Handwriting

- Reduce need for handwriting.
    a. Do not have child recopy material; it will get progressively worse instead of better.
    b. Allow student to copy a peer's notes or the teacher's notes.
    c. Accept typed or taped assignments.
- Reduce standards on some assignments and make relevant standards clearer on important assignments.
    a. Color, circle, or underline parts of letters that children typically fail to close in cursive writing.
    b. Allow reduced standards for acceptable handwriting.
    c. Display particularly good samples of the child's work.

Principles of Remediation for Low Self-Esteem

- Generally recognize the child's strengths and efforts.
    a. Call attention to the child's strengths by allowing for a consistent time each day or week during which the child can display his or her talents.
    b. recognize that excessive activity can also mean increased energy and productivity.
    c. Recognize that bossiness can also be leadership potential.
    d. Recognize that attraction to novel stimulation can also lead to creativity.
- Increase feelings of success by helping the child increase his or her skills.
    a. Recognize the child's playfulness and use it to develop skills.
    b. Mark the child's correct performance, not the mistakes.

References

American Psychiatric Association. (1987). *Diagnostic and statistical manual of mental disorders* (3rd ed., revised). Washington, DC: Author.

Chalfant, J. C., Pysh, M., & Moultrie R. (1979). Teacher assistance teams: A model for within building problem solving. *Learning Disabilities Quarterly, 2*(3), 85–96.

Council of Administrators of Special Education. (1992). *Student access: A resource guide for educators.* Albuquerque, NM: Author.

Davila, R. R., Williams, M. L., & MacDonalt, J. T. (1991). *Clarification of policy to address the needs of children with attention deficit disorders within general and/or special education.* Washington, DC: U.S. Department of Education, Office of Special Education and Rehabilitation Services.

Forness, S. R., & Walker, H. M. (1991a). Classroom systems and strategies for attention deficit disorders. (Part 1). *Challenge, 5*(4), 1–4.

Forness, S. R., & Walker, H. M. (1991b). Classroom systems and strategies for attention deficit disorders. (Part 2). *Challenge, 5*(5), 3–5.

Fowler, M. (1991, November). Testimony to CEC Task Force on Children with Attention Deficit Disorder, New Orleans.

Guetzloe, E. (1991, November). Testimony to CEC Task Force on Children with Attention Deficit Disorder, New Orleans.

Interagency Committee on Learning Disabilities. (1987). *Learning disabilities: A report to the U.S. Congress.* Washington, DC: Author. (ED294 358)

Kalan, M. R. (1991). *Superintendent's Task Force report on attention deficit disorder.* Ft. Lauderdale, FL: Broward County Public Schools.

Kelly, D. P., & Aylward, G. P. (1992). Attention deficits in school-aged children and adolescents. *Pediatric Clinics of North America, 39*(3), 487–512.

Kendall, K. C., & Braswell, L. (1982). Cognitive-behavioral self control therapy for children: A components analysis. *Journal of Consulting and Clinical Psychology, 50*(5), 672–689.

Michener, F. E. (1991). *Adolescent attention deficit disorders.* Alexandria, VA: Author.

Ortiz, A. A. (1991, November). Testimony before the CEC Task Force on children with Attention Deficit Disorders, New Orleans.

Parker, H. (1992). *The ADD hyperactivity handbook for schools.* Plantation, FL: Impact.

Popper, C. W. (1991). ADD look-alikes. *CHADDER, 5*(3), 16.

Professional Group for ADD and Related Disorders (PGARD). (1991). *Response from PGARD to the Congressional Notice of Inquiry on ADD.* Unpublished manuscript.

Reeve, R. E. (1990). ADHD: Facts and fallacies. *Intervention in School and Clinic, 26*(2), 70–78.

Reeve, R. E. (May, 1992). Personal communication.

Spessard, M. (April, 1992). Personal communication.

Thousand, J. S., & Villa, R. A. (1990). Strategies for educating learners with severe disabilities within their local home schools and communities. *Focus on Exceptional Children, 23*(3), 1–24.

Virginia Department of Education Task Force (1990). *Attention deficit hyperactivity disorder and the schools.* Richmond: Virginia Department of Education.

Zentall, S. S. (1991a, September). *School and family factors that improve outcomes for ADHD youth.* Paper presented at the third annual Children with Attention Deficit Disorders conference, Washington, DC.

Zentall, S. S. (1991b, November). Testimony to CEC Task Force on Children with Attention Deficit Disorder, New Orleans.

Additional Resources

As mentioned in the introduction, we hope that this booklet will serve as a starting point for educational personnel in their efforts to make the programs, policies, and procedures of their schools more conducive to fully meeting the educational needs of children with ADD. Again, the programs and interventions described in this document are not necessarily the "best" practices, nor are they the only practices currently being used with children with ADD in schools today. If your school is in the process of developing or modifying programs or policies in order to better meet the needs of children with ADD (or other children whose educational difficulties may put them at risk of school failure), we suggest you obtain further information from the sources listed here.

Federally Funded Centers on ADD

The 1990 Amendments to IDEA directed the Department of Education to provide funds to support one or more centers designed to organize, synthesize, and disseminate current knowledge relating to children with ADD. The purpose of these centers is to help educators, researchers, and parents respond to the needs of children with ADD and to provide access to the current research knowledge base related to either (a) assessment and identification or (b) intervention. Four centers have been funded, two addressing each issue. The centers and project directors are as follows:

Intervention

Dr. James Swanson
University of California–Irvine
19262 Jamboree Boulevard
Irvine, CA 92715
(714) 856-8730

Dr. Tom Fiore
Research Triangle Institute
3040 Cornwallis Road
P.O. Box 12194
Research Triangle Park, NC 27709
(919) 541-6004

Assessment and Identification

Dr. James McKinney
University of Miami
P.O. Box 248065
Coral Gables, FL 33124
(305) 284-5389

Dr. Roscoe Dykman
Department of Pediatrics
Arkansas Children's Hospital
    Research Center
1120 Marshall Street
Little Rock, AR 72202-3591
(501) 320-3333

In addition to these four centers, support has been granted to the Federal Resource Center to identify successful practices and programs, both in special education and in regular education, for meeting the educational needs of children with ADD. For further information, contact

Dr. Larry Carlson
Federal Resource Center
University of Kentucky
314 Mineral Industries Building
Lexington, KY 40506
(606) 257-1337

Information on ADD may also be obtained through the following national parent support organizations:

CH.A.D.D.
Children with Attention
 Deficit Disorders
499 N.W. 70th Avenue, Suite 308
Plantation, FL 33317
(305) 587-3700

ADDA
Attention Deficit Disorder
 Association
P.O. Box 488
West Newbury, MA 01895

Other organizations that may provide useful information to both parents and education personnel include

ERIC Clearinghouse for
 Handicapped and Gifted
 Children
The Council for Exceptional
 Children
1920 Association Drive
Reston, VA 22091
(703) 264-9474

NICHCY
National Information Center
 for Children and Youth
 with Handicaps
P.O. Box 1492
Washington, DC 20013
1-(800) 999-5599

LDA
Learning Disabilities Association
 of America
4156 Library Road
Pittsburgh, PA 15234
(412) 341-1515

NPND
National Parent Network on
 Disabilities
1600 Prince Street, Suite 115
Alexandria, VA 22314
(703) 684-6763

NASP
National Association of School
 Psychologists
8455 Colesville Road, Suite 1000
Silver Spring, MD 20910
(301) 608-0500

The following resources were used as sources for the Task Force report, and they may be particularly useful for school personnel:

Student Access. A resource guide for educators containing information on the rights, protection and services available to students under Section 504 of the Vocational Rehabilitation Act of 1973, and the Individuals with Disabilities Education Act of 1990. Available from the Council of Administrators of Special Education, Inc., 615 - 16th Street, NW, Albuquerque, NM 87104. Phone: (505) 243-7622.

The ADD Hyperactivity Handbook for Schools, Harvey C. Parker. Details strategies for identifying and teaching students with attention deficit disorder in elementary and secondary schools. Contains worksheets that may be reproduced for use in classrooms. Published by Impact Publications, Inc., 300 N.W. 70th Avenue, Plantation, FL 33317. Phone: (305) 792-8944.

Task Force Report: Attention Deficit Hyperactivity Disorder and the Schools. Available from the Virginia Department of Education, Richmond, VA 23216

Attention Deficit Disorders: A Guide for Teachers. Available from CH.A.D.D., Children with Attention Deficit Disorders, 499 N.W. 70th Avenue, Suite 308, Plantation, FL 33317. Phone: (305) 587-3700.

Additional ADD Resources

Facing the Challenges of ADD: A Kit for Parents and Educators, Chesapeake Institute. Includes two video tapes, Facing the Challenges of ADD (a 30-minute video directed primarily to parents), and One Child in Every Classroom (an hour-long video that provides effective teaching strategies). The package also includes a Users Guide, an extensive directory of materials, and several reproducible fact sheets. # M5105 1995 $50.

Teaching Strategies: Education of Children with Attention Deficit Disorder, Chesapeake Institute. Help for general educators and parents who are trying to understand and teach students with ADD. The book gives teachers examples of techniques they can use. # P5076 1994 38 pp. $8.90.

How to Reach and Teach ADD/ADHD Children: Practical Techniques, Strategies, and Interventions for Helping Children with Attention Problems and Hyperactivity, Sandra F. Rief. This complete resource is like having an expert at your side to answer virtually any question on how to work with children with learning disabilities or attention problems, or with children who are underachieving for any number of reasons. Tells how to teach organization and study skills as well as multisensory strategies for teaching reading, writing, and math. # S391 1993 245 pp. $27.95.

ADHD: Inclusive Instruction and Collaborative Practices, Sandra F. Rief. Following a brief discussion of ADHD, this video demonstrates successful practices and proven techniques. # M5085 1994 38 min/VHS $110.

Issues in the Education of Children with Attention Deficit Disorder. *Exceptional Children,* Special Issue, Vol. 60, No. 2. This special issue presents information on educational implications, diagnostic indicators, educational assessment, neurological basis, effect of stimulant medication, and promising school-based practices. # B5022 1993 96 pp. $8.50.

Call for the most current price and availability information: 1- 800-CEC-READ (232-7323).